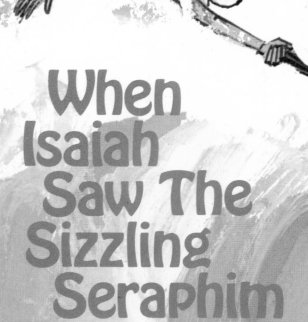

When Isaiah Saw The Sizzling Seraphim

Words by Norman C. Habel
Pictures by Jim Roberts

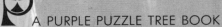

A PURPLE PUZZLE TREE BOOK

COPYRIGHT © 1972 CONCORDIA PUBLISHING HOUSE, ST. LOUIS, MISSOURI
CONCORDIA PUBLISHING HOUSE LTD., LONDON, E. C. 1
MANUFACTURED IN THE UNITED STATES OF AMERICA

ISBN 0-570-06523-2

Concordia Publishing House

One day Isaiah sat
and slowly watched a vision
of God inside His temple,
high above the heaven.
There God sat upon His throne
and shimmered full of light
as red rays spun around Him,
hot and wild and bright.

And sizzling seraphim,
like flying silver snakes,
flashed their neon wings
and filled the sky with flakes
of fluttering orange light.

And as they flew they sang:

Are you sleeping?
Are you sleeping?
Isaiah! Isaiah!
God is in His temple!
God is in His temple!
Calling you!
Calling you!

Holy, holy! Holy, holy!
Lord of hosts!
Lord of hosts!
Can you see His glory?
Can you see His glory?
Shining there.
Everywhere.

When God spoke, the temple shook
and thunder rocked the sky:
"I AM YAHWEH! I AM!" said God,
"JUST WHO ARE YOU, YOUNG MAN?"

Lumps of bright, red smoke
kept tumbling down like chips.
"I'll die! I'll die!"
Isaiah cried,
"for I have seen the Lord,
and I have dirty lips."

Then one of the sizzling seraphim
flew with a flit
to the altar pit
and snatched a glowing coal,
snarling hot…
SSSSSSSSOT!

He set the coal upon the tips
of Isaiah's dirty, lying lips.
God burned his lies away
and said, "You are forgiven.
You can stand this day
in front of all My fire,
for I have made you clean."

The Lord forgives us, too,
when we are scared
to face Him
because of lies we say or do.

Then all the seraphim
rose up to hear God speak:
"WHOM SHALL I SEND TODAY
TO TELL THE PEOPLE BELOW ME
THAT I MUST PUNISH THEM
BECAUSE THEY WILL NOT LOVE ME?"

All of heaven was silent!
Not even the north wind blew.
No one spoke. No one whispered.
No one wanted to go! Would you?
Then up Isaiah jumped
like a little boy at school.
"I'll go! I'll go!" he yelled,
"I'll be Your little fool."

Well, no one liked to hear the message
of this prophet from the skies.
They didn't want to learn
God hated all their lies.
Then one day Isaiah
went to visit the king,
a rat of a king called Ahaz,
who did many a rat-like thing!

He told King Ahaz not to fear
the enemy called Syria,
for God would soon deliver him
if he would only believe.
"Ask me for a sign," Isaiah said,
"and I will make it clear
that God can save His people,
for God is very near."

But Ahaz was a rat
who said he wouldn't
bother God
by asking for a silly sign
or anything like that.

Do you know where to look
for signs of God on high?
Along the road?
Or in a race?
Across the sky?
Or in your mother's face?

Isaiah told King Ahaz
that God had made a sign,
and the king had better listen
instead of drinking wine.
The sign was a lovely lady
and the baby she would carry,
a boy with the name Immanuel
instead of Tom, Dick, or Harry.

"Before that boy is four or five,"
said Isaiah to the king,
"the enemy who's bothering you
will hardly be alive,
and you will all be safe."

The sign came true
and Immanuel was born;
the enemy was beaten
and Israel was safe,
at least for a little while.

But the sign was like a signpost
pointing far ahead of them
to another lovely lady
and another Baby Boy
in the little town of Bethlehem.
Do you know their names?

For years Isaiah preached
and cried, "So says the Lord.
You'd better listen carefully
and keep His daily Word."
But no one ever listened
and no one really cared!

Soon another foe arrived,
the army of Assyria,
with miles and miles of soldiers
like miles and miles of serpents,
crying, "One Two, One Two!
We will kill you!"

This time the people were scared
and the king was scared as well.
But Isaiah had a message,
saying, "You will go to hell
and Jerusalem will be
just a pile of rubbish
unless you change your heart
and really trust in Me."

This king was Hezekiah
and he was a squeaky little guy,
but he prayed to God for help
and the Lord heard his cry.
That night there came a howl
like the screeching of an owl
as those miles and miles of soldiers,
like miles and miles of serpents,
crawled around the wall.
OOOOOOOOOOOOOOOOEEEEEEEEEE!

For God had sent His angel
with a horrible plague of deaths
that spread throughout the army
like a hundred thousand rats.

The enemy died on every side
as Israel sang its cry
of praise to God on high:

    We will praise You!
    We will praise You!
    God above! God above!
    When You come to save us!
    When You come to save us!
    By Your love!
    By Your love!

For years the people waited
for a king with might and fire—
not a rat like Ahaz
or little Hezekiah—
but someone greater than David,
who could save the people of God
from any evil anywhere,
no matter how fierce or odd!

And that promised King is the key
to the purple puzzle plan
for you and me.

Do you know His name?

OTHER TITLES

the PURPLE PUZZLE TREE